Leila's First Visit to the Dentist

Written by: Dr. Humairah Shah
Illustrations by: Javier C Gonzalez III

This Book Belongs to:

Leila was going to see the dentist.

"What is a dentist, mommy?" asked Leila.

"A dentist takes care of your teeth and makes sure they are nice and strong. The dentist also makes sure that no sugar bugs live in your mouth," explained Leila's mom.

At the dentist's office, there were other kids and parents too.

After a while, Susie, the nurse, took Leila and her mom to a room. It was a beautiful room and it reminded Leila of the zoo. There were colorful pictures of animals all around.

"Leila, I have to take some pictures of your teeth," said Susie.

Susie showed Leila the camera. It was a big blue camera, much bigger than the one Leila had at home.

Leila sat on a chair and Susie placed an apron with a big happy face on her. Leila took lots of pictures with the giraffe, bear and monkey.

"I am going to get your pictures ready and in the meantime, you can watch a movie," said Suzie.

"This place is fun," said Leila.

After a while, Susie took Leila to see Dr. Jane. Dr. Jane had Leila lie down on a chair. She had a magic mirror and a special tooth counter.

"I have to count your teeth and see if you have any sugar bugs in them," said Dr. Jane.

Leila opened her mouth big and wide like an alligator so Dr. Jane could have a good look at her teeth.

Dr. Jane looked for bugs with her magic mirror and counted them with the tooth counter. When she was done, she had a big smile on her face.

"Leila, you have twenty teeth and they are pretty clean and strong. There are no sugar bugs in your mouth," said Dr. Jane.

Dr. Jane reminded Leila that she had to brush her teeth for two minutes every morning and every night. She suggested Leila listen to her favorite song and brush from the time it starts till it ends.

"Do not forget to floss at night as well; sugar bugs love to hide between your teeth," said Dr. Jane.

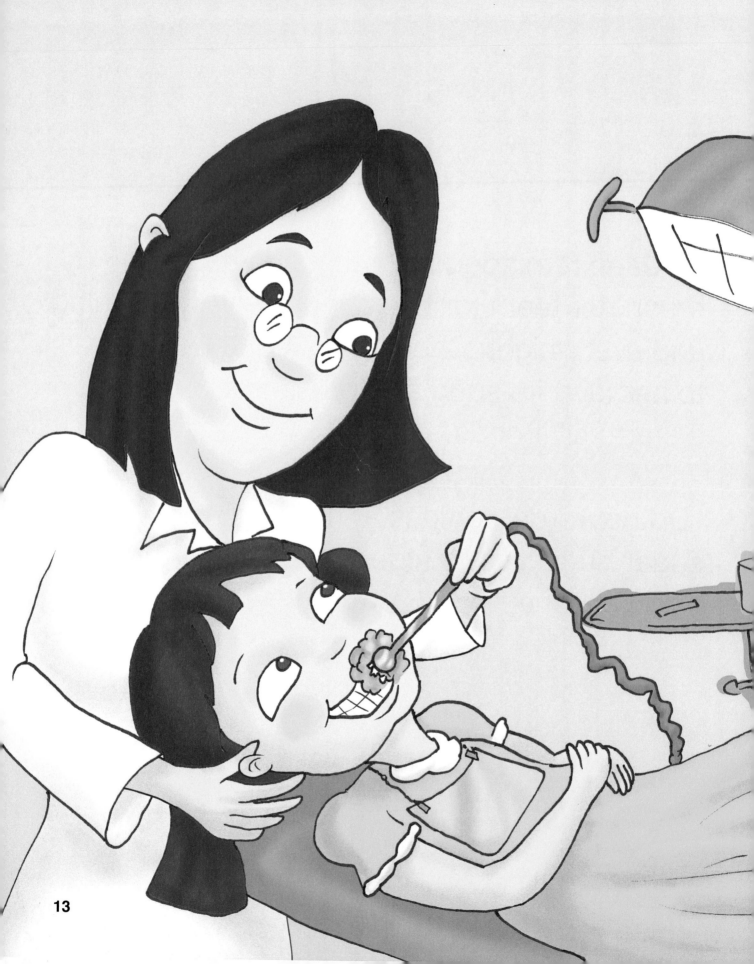

13

"Leila, I am going to brush your teeth now," explained Dr. Jane.

"Dr. Jane that toothbrush looks different," pointed out Leila.

"Yes it is. It's a very special toothbrush. It goes round and round and makes a *zzzzzzzzz* sound. Would you like the cherry or strawberry flavored toothpaste?" asked Dr. Jane.

"Cherry is my favorite," said Leila happily.

So Dr. Jane brushed Leila's teeth with the cherry toothpaste.

Dr. Jane's tooth brush was funny. It tickled Leila's teeth and made her laugh. Now that Leila was done, she got to pick two toys and a tooth brush.

"I love this place mommy and the dentist too! I want to come back and see Dr. Jane again," said Leila.

"Oh yes, we certainly will," said her mother.

My First Visit To the Dentist

[Paste Picture]

My Picture

[Paste Picture]

Other Books by the Author

Funny Teeth and Bunny Ears a story about thumbsucking, follows Charlie and Marlie on their wild adventure! Despite their mother's warnings they continue to suck their thumbs. The two find themselves in a pickle as the story unfolds!

Sam and the Sugar Bug is a story that educates children about the importance of brushing their teeth. The book also prepares children for having their teeth cared for by a dentist in a fun and engaging way.

Leila and the Tooth Fairy is a story that every parent would love to read to their kids when they lose their teeth. The book allows them to save the dates each time they lose a tooth. The story takes the kids to a magical Tooth Fairy Land, and in a fun and easy way educates them about eating a healthy diet.

Funny Teeth and **Bunny Ears**

By Dr. Humairah Shah
Illustrated by Adriana Clark

Sam and the Sugar Bug

Written by: Dr. Humairah Shah
Illustrations by: Javier C Gonzalez III

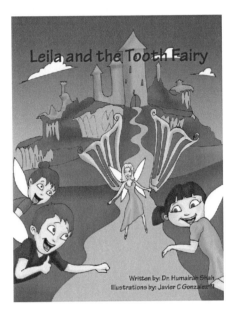

Leila and the Tooth Fairy

Written by: Dr. Humairah Shah
Illustrations by: Javier C Gonzalez III

Made in the USA
San Bernardino, CA
17 March 2019